To marty,

Always Believe
You Can!

Don
Blum
5/2023

Things I Couldn't Say until Today

A Romantic Journey Written in Verse
with Original Color Illustrations

Dave Black

Library of Congress Cataloging – in-Publication Data has been applied for.

ISBN: 978-1-66786-526-3
eBook ISBN 978-1-66786-527-0

Contents

Prologue

The ***Things I Couldn't Say Until Today*** is the accumulation of many years of writing down certain moments in time and trying to put them into verse much like artists in the music world. I have grown up admiring the clever use of words and the telling of stories in song. Artists like Al Stewart and Dan Fogelberg, who can tell a story in perfect, yet simple rhyme were key influences. And the master, Bob Dylan, who can paint a story complete with deep yet relatable verse to a beat. You were and still are my idols!

Unfortunately, I have never been able to carry a tune musically. Yet, I have embraced the notion that I too, "could" tell a story with verse that spoke about a moment in time and that I could get a message to rhyme. See, it's that easy if you try!

I started primitive efforts in writing while my mind was roaming during college lectures, when I should have been listening. I'm sure the professors would look and be pleased that I was taking copious notes at the time; what little did we both know.

That's how it started and soon after I was trying my hand at creating poems to express my feelings. These efforts were enhanced when I first fell in love. Honestly, I was able to share my feelings through my writings much better than I was verbally. Through the years following there were many shifts in relationships and fortunately I was able to chronicle my feelings in verse, capturing all the highs and lows.

Many of my thoughts were written in note form in need of polish. Some came to me as inspirations and quickly the words just flowed. Other poems were lying in wait, incomplete and took a fresh look years later before they were shaped into what they are now.

It wasn't until recently that I was able to put this into a theme and recreate my story in a way that is somewhat relatable to what many go through on their journey during their single days of dating.

Now I can share the Things I Couldn't Say!!!!

Benevolence

May your love
> Grow with friendship.

May your Friendship
> Reflect that love.

May your thoughts soar together
> Like a bird, ever free.

May you Fly onward as one
> And know not boundaries
>> As time descends.

With two sharing as one
> Life will always hold
>> A gift of kindness.

Written for a friend on his wedding day.

First Date

Curiosity running wild, those big blue eyes
Looking right through, without words, say'n so much
Melting my heart, am I ready for this surprise?
Much anticipation, these feelings I can touch.

Floating along, the conversation is light,
Teasing me, calling, like never before
As I look across at you, my thoughts take flight
These expressions are more than I could ask for.

Time beating fast, as my heart races open
Keep the rhythm going, yet play it slow
Send a signal, I want to let it show
a nod or something, even unspoken.

I look into your eyes and show you a sign
Hinting at more, we share a smile
I can be true, if you can spend more time
Can we be together longer than a while?

Your blue eyes take me, my feelings soar
Your smile, has me thinking, as I retreat
Warmed with desire, to know you more,
As I dream of the day our lips can meet.

Can we share a second date?

It's Time for Spring

The sun rises silently
With a new warming radiance
Cast over grains of sand
Like you and I, one in a million.

Lapping waves caress our thoughts
Baptizing each soul, with rebirth
As the timeless symmetry runs clear
Exposing a fancy for amorous ways.

As mystical as the longing to share
The tide chants a call of spring in the air
To drifters having witnessed the ebb
And await raptures' capturing wave.

When by chance we should meet
Artistically, the elegance will shine
As new horizons set sail amass
For her heart will be like an ocean
As I lie patiently on the shore.

Heaven in your Eyes

Have you ever asked yourself?
What's in heaven and why is it our goal
While living on earth?

I think of heaven as the smiles you give
The emotions you show
The person you are
Without trying to be.

With this crystal-clear vision
In your eyes I can see
Just how it's a goal,
As you set me free.

In you I have found heaven right next to me.

Our First Kiss

Cinnamon hair swaying
Carefree in the summer breeze
Casting a hint toward passion
As the sun shines amber in the forenoon.

Burgundy lips alive
With the moistness of morning dew
Smile as if they hold a longing
To touch this stranger.

Eyes of hazel, amid a verdant field
Open wide to look at one
Whose image she holds in mind
With reverence to the golden rule
The day has flourished primrose.

As the sun begins its subtle departure
The colors reflect an affinity
While we lie in the crimson shadow
And ponder our lips first meeting.

In shades of plum, our faces hold a content
Creating a poetic rainbow within
Thankful for the opalescent beauty
Of sharing our first kiss.

True Nature

Shimmering water, I can see
The reflection of your eyes.

Drifting clouds, I think of
Your smile as it lightens my day.

Gentle breeze, I fancy the scent
Of your perfumed waves of hair.

Curving hills, I reminisce of
The grace of your feminine charm.

Forest green and powder blue
Layers of color, surround my outlook
As I encounter nature's way.

Amidst warmth and freshness
Captured in silent display
I confide that you are the
True nature of my soul.

Because of You

Have you ever tried to fall in love
But it just didn't work out?
It can't be drawn out of you.

It just shines in their eyes
Saying you are beautiful
And you have freely chosen
To be with me.

Because of you, I'm alive with new feelings
Given only to you, knowing you feel the same
Lingers with me throughout each day
In every thought and everything I do
Comes right back to being with you.

Now I know what love feels like
All because of you!

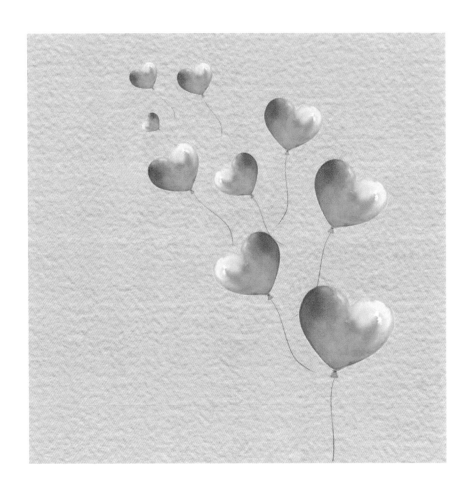

Our Simple Love

I love you honey, because
You provide me youth
Along the road to adulthood
We question it, hoping for proof.

You give it to me
Enclosed in your smile
As I know we'll stay together
Longer than a while.

Your love stays within me
As new feelings soar
Because you are all I ever
Want to care for.

This Magic Night Lingers

Our night is over so now I drive
Away from your door feeling so alive
The sound carries a beat to the song
On the radio with a rhythm ever so strong.

Your perfume is in the air, as I hold the wheel
Scents of this magic night linger and reveal
So, past your house I sail once again
to replay it all over, as my head starts to spin.

My senses alive, some call it love
I'm new to this feeling, I thank God above
I'll be up all night knowing this is not a sham
Thinking about how caught up in you I am.

Over and over, I replay that song
And to know you by heart, I wanted all along
To capture this moment right on cue
As I drift deeper in love with you.

Tomorrow I will float to your door
And we'll do it all over again!

Summers Wishes

We met by chance in the spring
And watched our love happen
You came on like heaven and wine
My sorrows just melted away with you.

In my heart there is a new song to sing
We came together on the first of May
And found happiness in simple ways
As our minds meshed together as one.

We stayed together through the summer days
Your love like a shadow, ever harder to define
The days rushed by like a warm breeze
Sharing it all, we left nothing behind.

As we toss our coins into the well
We share our wishes together
Longing for more we embrace,
And hold on to this special time.

Can we make this last?

Prelude

Silent as the daybreak, she waits
Until her flower suddenly blooms
Enlightened by its fruit to bear.

So restless is he, careless the spores fall
Cast adrift with the spring wind
That one knows not where?

As twilight creeps near together we're still
Within the shadow encasing the earth
Unaware of how fertile tomorrow will be,
We ride this wave all we can.

Seeds implanted, sewn together with love
In the still of the mind's eye, we lie
Only to await dawns tying thread of life
Like thoughts of love not yet harvested.

My Brightest Star

This star lit night holds my love
Like a dream so real is the hope
Yet, out of reach the reality sets in
And I am watching its dim light fade.

As I still look to the heavens
And wonder where you are
In thinking about you I believe

That no matter how far you wander
You are right here with me
My Brightest Star.

Water Color

Your love is like a water color rainbow
Against the pouring rain I see
The spirit and light you cast
And how everything flows together
Into one beautiful being.

I am not worthy of such a treasure
As I thank my lucky stars
That you walked into my life
And taught me the meaning of magic.

For your love has painted a picture
One brush stroke at a time
On how I want to live.

My Thanks to You (a Love Song)

I want to thank you
for answering the door
And letting me into your life
For I've been waiting at the doorstep
Searching for someone with open arms.

I want to tell you
How you've rebuilt my broken dreams
Into reality once again
With the laughter and smiles
And the heartbeats we share.

I want to let you know
How you fill my every wish
For life has been so beautiful
And each day brings a special meaning.

I want to whisper
My thanks to you
For being the way, you are
And as I speak
Only three words can be said!

I'm Going to Say it

Often, I want to write something new
Maybe something sweet about me and you
But God it's hard even though I try
All I get is a question as I look to the sky.

Why is it that I care so much?
That everything I do
Was meant and given just for you.

As my day passes slowly, waiting for tonight
When I get to see you again
I am left holding my dreams of how it's true
And I just can't wait any longer
to say the words, I love you!

An Early Morning Prayer

Begin each day with thanks
For the chance to breathe a new.

Focus your thoughts toward the kindness
Bursting forth in your heart.

Sing the song of bliss with the harmony
Expounding from your soul.

Lighten the day, shed the glistening rays
Of your smile to someone who is near.

I awoke this morning, silently in prayer
Just watching as you sleep

Thanking God for you!

Tonight's Sky

Harvest moon delight, puritan ways
Why look back, when you can look through,
And fall deeply in love
With tonight's brilliant sky.

The waxing moon travels
as waning thoughts set sail
To a place on the horizon clear
Searching the stars for signs of you.

And finally, I spot you above
For you are with me tonight
Memory my forever friend.

Windy Day Thoughts

Rolling waves, air full of sound
Changing skies, brace yourself
For this day is bound for drifting,
So best to hold your ground.

Stay with this strong-willed breeze
Expand horizons for pure joy, not need
Look for adventure that buckles your knees
And create new memories freed from routine.

A chance to escape it howls profound
Unclear are the thoughts just blowing by
For those who are stranded with indecision
Uncertain to what this windy day brings.

Skipping Stones

Bright summer day, sun kissed skies,
Skipping stones from the shore
Carbonated waves calling me.

I think and wonder as stones fly
On how the skeptics say why,
And the dreamers why not.

But on this random day
There seems like nothing better
To do than ponder a way
Of how to approach you,

As I count the ripples.

A Cold Fall Night

Autumns late air blowing cold
The curtain falls with sunsets early
Foreshadowing winds come forth
Leaves scattering one last time.

It gets me wondering, am I ready
To reflect as darkness creeps in
Narrowing my choices to make
Have I stored enough to survive,

These long nights ahead without you.

Fog

Feeling dense, the clouds aren't lifting,
Mind bogged down, same thoughts drifting,
like the swells on the shore wandering,
Rolling over and over, I'm pondering.

Failing to form the conclusion I want
So, I could breathe fresh without haunt
That would change something gone by
to release this haze gone awry.

It goes on and on.

The foghorn sounds, no other ships in sight
No peril, not lost, just can't see the light
Where is the beacon to guide me to the shore?
And find safe harbor, from this maelstrom
of no direction, just endless waves of plight.

Will this fog ever lift?

Last Stop

Standing at the crossroads
Derailed train of thought
No words can describe
This emptiness deep inside.

Eyes cast drifting away
There's not a chance to stay
As the evening shadows cast
Over the feelings of the past.

There's nothing more to say
Best to just walk away
No chance to say what's
Still in my heart.

We are miles apart!

Whether or Not?

Dark clouds rising, swirling skies gray,
There's stormy weather brewing
No denying, there's something wrong
Conditions sure do change fast.

You can feel it in the air
Pressure on all fronts collide
With feelings buried, so hard to now share
What's really happening before it's too late.

In my mind there's no storm we can't weather
If we can hang on, we'll ace this test
For in time, this too shall pass, will you?
Can you take shelter in the foundation,
On which our commitment lies?

Unsure if we can handle turbulent weather
The sirens wail, warning only at the last minute
before recking its dreaded havoc
Shellshocked, this storm had left us severely damaged.

I'm left in its wake, wondering
Whether or not, I was worth it
Or was I merely a fair-weather love.

Another Morning

Mourners always seem to find one another
With their arms held open
For the one who has left.

Sympathy reigns, yet the skies are dry
Like tears not yet shed.

For you there is no wrong
     Only your right,
And when you've found him
Hold on to the night.

For another morning you may awake
To find your own arms left open.

Sunset in the Shadows

Watching the sunset by myself
I am left in the twilight's shadows
Advancing darkness feeling so alone.

The sun is leaving, without a promise,
Will it return?
Are you the same,
Lost amidst the shadows?

The colors and hues blend
In their subtle way
While night's clouds run free
Reflecting over the changes
Which always seem to creep in.

Lately I've wondered why
Every sunset leaves us further apart
And if the sun will ever rise
On our love again?

For a Lost Love

Full of regret I am longing for you
I find you in every idle daydream
I have never stopped loving you
Yet through this shell of hidden feelings
I can never admit it to you.

Like a car in need of a push
You started my engine just being yourself
Only now do I realize that you're the key
To what's locked away deep inside of me.

Yet for now I can only wish
That you'll come on home
And free my heart from the chains
Of not showing more love to you.

Why can't I just tell you this?

Crushed

It's such a rush when you allow a crush
To take over your thinking.
The future allows for daring rewards
Always at the expense of something safe.

No risk, no reward
You are entitled to play this game
With the fear of missing out unsaid
Why sadly, is it at my expense?

You will never know the full extent
The weight your decision carries
And like an anvil, falling from the sky
Its impact has just CRUSHED me.

Erosion

So gradual is the decay, one hardly notices
Subtle in its way, how things evolve
For day to day it starts, quietly withdrawn
Unaware of the sea change foretold.

Waves hitting the shore with unending attrition
A beat so faint one feels no threat
Its theme unscathed, we are blind to witness
So tiny are the break downs, yet cracks in the seams.

In time we began to drift further a part
Without a way to talk, no heart-to-heart
Unable to recognize its affect, like us
It doesn't make itself clear.

Its only after the results occur, can you feel
The abrasion of which the sands of time bring
For over and over it had worn away
The layers of love we had built on a string,

Now depositions have permanently changed
So large is the breach, we can never get it back
for erosion is clear only after it occurs
Leaving a gap too big for us to fill.

Right before our eyes, our Love had washed away.

Aftermath

Looking out gazing over the bridge
The water is still the same gently flowing
Like the love we let drift away.

The pain is gone, but the aftermath remains
Without a glance to the other side.

Empty feelings immersed in silence
Never to be washed ashore.

The tide waivers solemnly
Like a lover's hope
Lost, without destiny.

In Days of Rebound

Morning = Hope
Afternoon = Faith
Evening = Uncertain
Night = ALONE!
REPEAT

With no hands on the wheel, I spin
In circles until time moves ahead.

Can I navigate through this cycle
And steer through these endless waves,
To reach a place with distance traveled
Where I can begin to rebuild?

Long are the empty days until I meet someone new.

Fragments of Smoke

There's smoke in the distance, its haze forms a ghost.
That hangs on as the days still haunt.
It's all that's left from what we had,
Unable to vanish at this time, it stands slow.

The smoke lingers, as the flame dies out
Left only are embers of what used to warm us so.
My tears dowse the fire until it's no more
Just like feelings she once had.

Still, you wonder where these feelings went
And why do they still burn in my heart
Leaving me shivering from the cold
As the faint smell of smoke dissipates.

In the morning when I wake
Only ashes remain to remind me
just how empty I feel.

One Year ago, Today

I never thought I'd be here
Alone in shadows cast near
Where are the smiles we shared?
Where is the way we once cared?

Somewhere captured inside
Are feelings we both can't hide
If time wouldn't run, maybe you could see
The way it was just one year ago.

I thought you would always stay
But love, like a windy day
Has its part to play
In life's ever-changing way.

Those times I've cried
Are the times I tried
To see through loves' disguise
Instead of looking to your eyes.

Dodging reflections as I wake
With so much love to make
I live to find someone new
Yet all I can think of is you.

Can we ever find a way
Back into each other's heart?
And relive that feeling, as love restarts
Just like it was one year ago today.

Another Phase of Loneliness

Deep in a summer's night, I walked
Along the beach and then sat
Thinking of midnights gone by
Thoughts just out of reach.

I watched the moon travel
Luminating the crystalline water
As a young couple walks hand in hand
A silhouette of nights long past.

Drowning in the essence of pale light
Another phase of loneliness enters
Feeling numb as it comes to mind
Where there is shadow, there is light.

And on a star my wish is made
With a longing to know her name
As each night passes unwed
My wish becomes more of a prayer.

The Things I Couldn't Say (until today)

After all this time I could never find the words to say
How I felt, until I woke up to the sounds of today.
All these years, so many tears, always left behind
Haunting me, a prisoner, locked within my mind.

What brings this on today, you may ask
Why do I now want to take off this mask?
That held feelings bound inside so long ago
And release them now, from their place in tow.

Buried deep inside the chains on my heart
There lies an honesty I just can't depart
How hard it was to vanish and not say
That I miss you, as part of my every day.

And now that I'm here, If I can stay in this place
Where I believe in God's giving grace
And know you missed me once too
I could forgive myself for the ways
I failed to show my love for you.

Back On the Run

I've been standing still way too long
Jogging on an endless treadmill within
Conditioned to believe its limits
Without my minds freedom to create.

Nature contends freedom will run
Nearer than one can imagine
For escape is only a step away
Just out the door lies the chance.

With inspiration I must get back on the run
And rebuild a strength through out
As my heart and soul expose my need.

As spring comes, the atmosphere is light
Given freely to support us
As I begin to breathe a new.

Seeing people while in motion
Frees my mind, refreshed
So clear as I tire
Knowing that life is no longer standing still!

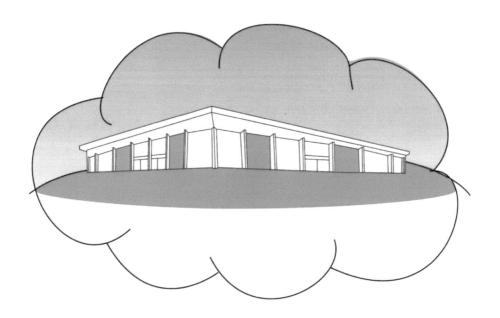

So Glad We MET
(ode to the Days of Met Center)

A drive past 494 and Cedar is not complete I am told
As one can see majestic white pillars towering over flat land bold
Without a second look as you can still see where it stood
It seems like yesterday; Met Center was what made life good.

Oh, what those hallowed Met Center halls could tell
With seats green, gold, black and white that stood proud in salute
To a pristine sheet of ice logoed for our North Stars in tribute
Over a quarter century, a campus and fraternity, you served us well.

Concert moments hang like smoke in the spotlighted air
Distorted sounds bounce as "A Stairway to Heaven" blares
Over a pot scented, beer spilled arena a shadow is cast
Illuminated by hundreds of lighters, in harmony, stoned a mass.

GLAMOR "ous" servants, we saw it all, from our operational view
We emerged so enriched, having been introduced by you
To the people we have come to know, caught in the same net
We gather to this day because of times spent at the MET.

One can still see it standing along that road, no mirage
As in the mind's eye the Met Center never fell
For every nook n cranny, stairwell, team room or club,
There remains a view so vivid, I see it clearly still.

There's never been a place so aptly named
Met Center, you were the center of everyone we met.
I Love you, all the Days of the Met Center
Let's raise a glass to toast and say, "So Glad We MET."

Wild Oats

One by one the days collide
As carefree as the fields we play
With friends aside we boast and toast
to our tales and how they unfold.

Thinking only of yourself and now
Late night carousing, a cat on the prowl
Driven, as no terms were ever written
At times we get smitten, by the wonder of it all.

Strange is this calling, absurd we chase
A party in a minute, no time to pace
Somehow you know this phase is racing
And where you will end up baffles us all.

Somehow you get thru the urge
To sow your crops by night, these wild oats
When, by accident you find one who stays
No more fields left to plow.

When you look back at how selfish you were
Unsaid, is what you have left in its wake
As you begin to grow and believe that fate
Has mysteriously led you to a harvest of lasting love.

For a Drifter

The breeze at your back,
you drift along the shore, wondering
should you take a chance
and open up the door.

One can feel the summer waves warming
Teasing your senses, so alive are thoughts
Growing deeper, one may choose to stray
in the heat of this sunny day.

Like sand in a glass, the hour is ours
If we can believe in this moment
For drifters who dare to say
Let's take a chance before time slips away.

Bridge The Gap

Do you remember or dare to admit feelings kind
Exiled deep and true, locked by our place in time?
Though our voyage was short, its impacts profound
Can we reconnect and make up ground?

For distance, like a river, has grown ever so long
Bound with evolution the swells are strong
In blocking out things that didn't go as planned
For no one lives untarnished, ahead of God's plan.

If we can find a way to release the levee encased
That holds thoughts dammed, locked in place,
And admit our shortfalls and come to arrive,
In a place of reflection, so calm and alive?

With class and grace ever thankful we reached
A place overflowing, the waters are breached.
For memories glossed over no longer left in haste.
We raise a glass and toast; they lie not in waste.

A special place this gateway lies, unabridged
Content in knowing it wasn't a waste of time.

Can we bridge the gap?

A Change of Season

As the door of time converges on autumn
I see what we shared, as leaves flaunt their colors
For what is held feels real and not ready to fall
Yet, can no longer beat openly in heart.

It's a strange way we live on a limb
And some of the unity becomes lost
Even the affinity which introduced us
Leaves to wonder, Was it ever really true?

With paths drawn in different directions
We continue in pursuit of our dreams
Yet, I have found a peace in knowing
You were once my reality.

If ever a reason our trails should cross
With this change of season, I'm open
And trust that you will be too
Because, you were once everything to me.

True colors surround my golden view
As the door is left ajar, holding this moment
Tempting fate, as the leaves hang on
Reminiscent of all we shared in time.

If ever a reason!

Illusions

Like a mirage on a clear day
Her smile condescends
Melting like the image of Venus
Then disappears.

As radiant as a summer's sunrise
Inspiring, yet ever harder to hold
Faith wanders amidst the shadows cast
Searching for a place to shine for one another.

Ready to stand witness I wait
For the day ever elusive,
That day I can look in her eyes
And meet the light of a new shared love.

Last Fall Campfire

The sky fades to grey earlier now
With a growing chill that reveals November is here
Yet the fires warmth brings rays of hope
As our hearts are open, ready to share once again.

The crackles and sounds make music in the night
Burning away the last of the leaves, as fall fades
It is ever clear as we gather, smoldering with purpose
We toast and enjoy one last fall campfire.

With you by my side, we are one with the flame
Darting to and fro, spirits alive, we embrace
Inspiring a new vision, over once pensive days
As soon snow will be in the air.

We watch the flame as it flickers
The sparks fly like snow flurries in the air
A foreshadowing of days to come,
We welcome the cold on our backs together.

Sharing our last fall campfire, we quietly witness
The warmth of our new love!

Snow Flurries

Temperature falling, gathering clouds create
An atmosphere nostalgic
As the first snow flurries appear.

And like memories flowing
In a blink of your eyes and they're gone.

Where did you go
Without a hint, so blurry
Like the way you came.

Vanished without warning
It leaves me wondering
Why You couldn't stay.

Winter Land

The snow gently glides
Unguided as it descends
Illuminated with a satin freshness
To cast a hint of the spirit above.

Newly fallen, with its velvet blanket
Lingering over an arcade of trees
Clinging to every branch and limb
Covering its quiet landscape.

Pure and welcome in seasonal delight
The picture is drawn with radiant innocence
Painted in solitude, as his love shines
While the author prefers to remain anonymous.

This Full Moon Winter's Night

On this full moon winter's night
With air so crisp
I ask, which direction is right
As I find myself adrift.

Warmed with your grace and spirit
Sounds so alive, I can hear it
As I travel this snow-covered road
Unsure of the path I should hold.

There's too much distance to cover
with travels back in time you hover
over this the chance you dare to take
Wondering, is this just another mistake?

Full of reflections, competing with now
with each step I make, will it allow
me to get closer and nearer to this
or am I merely falling into the abyss?

Inspired horizons, under this moonlit glow
overshadowing my fears, to this I owe
A prayer to focus my sight
For the vision to lead me ahead,
Can I see your guiding light?

Such are the trials, on this full moon winter's night.

The Fog is Lifting

New day, the fog is lifting
My clouded mind is clearing
Thoughts untangled are drifting
Away from sorrow endearing

Me to say,

Even if I had done things differently and changed
outcomes in a way, or by a step or two
It's better reflecting back, than life rearranged
As scattered thoughts once dense, come sifting through

My mind so true,

As God has granted serenity on this day
to begin and see a new me rising
From a journey back in time far away,
To a better place of understanding
With its healing ray forever baptizing

My soul anew,

Refreshed beyond an insatiable thirst
That twists the roads and their paths
To my favor, that always puts me first
Ahead of my love that lasts.

A Special Kind

Whenever I reflect on memories of those good old days
A smile crosses my face, as I race to the sky
Forgetting the aftermath of painful ways
Because you are a lady of a special kind.

A sadness comes to follow as my mind wanders,
Unsure if we can match these feelings again
And see how life's trail has led us here.

For now, we'll just have to wait
As I'm tethered until your smile returns
And if we can reach that day
It too will be fine as we will soar to the clouds.

Because, you are a lady of a special kind.

First Signs of Spring

The sun breaks over the horizon
As traces of frost melt, hints of dew
While winter steps aside and listens
To the purity of this morning's song.

Awaiting a new lease on life we witness
The first flower peaking its way above ground
While a robin cackles a greeting to all
Announcing his arrival.

As the last snow fades across the fields soft,
The first signs of Spring blooms clear
While our coat of hibernation vanishes,
Enlightening everyone as a sign of rebirth.

Today is the first day spring has arrived!

The Perfect Shell

As I walk along the beach, the sands of time
Are sifting through my steps in rhyme
The waves cascading, are washing the shore
Leaving us souvenirs from days before.

I search to capture my feelings to tell
And on the sand, there lies a shell
etched in fossil, an image from a bygone day
A match without any words needed to say.

And now that I've found the perfect shell
That echoes the feelings we once shared
The imprint you made, time can now tell
As I have finally found a way to say thank you!

I Wish You Well

Today is ending in its usual way
With you there and me here
Nothing new to say.

The evening rain lightly patters
On the windows of our minds
Searching for a spot free of pain
And full of content, the rainbow forms.

Yesterday's wind has blown across the path
With laughter stirring the sands of time
Into moments relived so clear in mind.

If my freedom is hingent on these memories,
I become a slave, parched with a thirst
To return to a place of peace
Where the words would make sense.

Tomorrow will arrive in an unusual way
With a new light that will shine as
Selfless as a summer breeze
With smiles remembering the affinity we shared
The words come finally out as a prayer….

Saying that I wish you well!

When I get There

Standing on the shore watching the waves
No pain, just empty, as vacant is my heart
Reflection is my face, as time just goes on
Until I take the plunge and trust again.

The water inviting leads me to try
Another journey about to set sail afloat
As I know there's someone there waiting
To be my guide and navigate the same boat.

Time is cold when your alone
But as sunny skies warm, I trust
They will lead me to you
And when I get there, we will both know.

A Better Plan (Near MRS.)

With the wind at your back, set sail a mast
What distance you travel, leaving the past
As if God intended, you were blown away
Drawn to a new journey, somewhere beyond today.

For you it's all about changing
Things up, instead of rearranging
For I cannot see what fate has in store
Pulling on heartstrings, I'm anchored to the shore.

So let the wind blow away these dreams
For we are two ships, each on their own course
Although we came close, we did not collide in time
Creating another of many near misses.

Who is this woman I'm hoping to find?
A part of a better plan undefined,
Where fate shows up and guides my ship
And I am not left to harbor a feeling of loss
For all of the ones who tied other knots.

I await God's better plan with faith that you will find me.

True Loves So Few

There are so few people that one can say
They have meant "I love you" in every way
Over time it unfolds an intrigue special
Unlike anything else we ever hold.

So why do we hide behind the facade
And pretend it didn't exist, numbers so small
Instead of embracing the memories
That once meant everything and all.

Are we bound to just block it and go about
Beneath the drag of how it didn't turn out
The way we thought it would back then
And can we see it clearly again?

I choose to treasure the times we had
Those building blocks, now pillars
On how we live and what we hold close
Less fickle the hands of fate over time.

For mature love has a place to hold
With respect those who came before
And taught us to re-open our hearts
As these thoughts are not easily told.

True loves so few there are in your life
Grants you to cherish one final gift
Which shapes us as days go forth
The memories of love past, held silently in heart.

Can we find the right place?

Enough

Yesterday my heart was so full
Yet today I start all over once again,
With a fresh chance to start anew
And see what CHARITY I can bring.

Am I ready to dodge obstacles as they appear?
The meter's running, am I spinning my wheels,
Or am I bringing the best that I can,
For that's all I can HOPE to do.

As advice long ago rings true,
Try to show the best of you
With the most love you can share
And let the rest go on FAITH.

If I do just that, it's certainly enough for me.
Will it be enough for you?

Sharing Hands

We walk around the lake
So much in our view
Admitting my feelings
Is really something new.

As you take my hand
We walk as one
And you tell me what you think
As we stop for a kiss.

Your beauty is like the universe
So mystical and baffling
Holding hands, we reach beyond
All mystery with this simple expression.

Our steps are light
As I float without boundary
My heart is pounding
With a rainbow of love for you.

Worth the Wait

She waited long for me
I awaited her love
Never known a feeling like it
Must be sent from heaven above.

Our love grew on softer
As quietly the waves serenade our view
With the spring breeze on our backs
We are living a dream come true.

The ocean view panoramic
Is so worth the wait
Surrounded in colors and hues
As our love grows with every date!

I'm Falling for you

There's a freshness I feel
Every time I am with you
Perhaps a thread tying
Us ever closer in our feelings.

Learning every minute just how
Much you mean to me, I am stranded
Without words, so much more
Then a crush blown by the wind

So much that in everything I do
comes out with a bouquet of thoughts
On how much I'm falling in love with you!

Ever Flowing

Fragments of thought lie captured
Beneath a moonlit sky
Summoned to the brink, like waters of spring
Retaped, can our feeling grow strong?

Reflections formed in parody
That excite this longing
To bring memories into
Feelings reborn in spirit

Inside lies the quiet souvenir
Given graciously from your heart
That my soul cannot wash away
This ever-flowing memory of you.

Coming Home

Coming home has many meanings,
What can I bring back, experiences learned?
That will help me ahead and share
And be a better person for our journey.

The roads have directions for us to take
Many curves and forks, decisions to make
For the way we want to live ahead
With a new energy that excites our view.

Leave a light in the window and say a prayer
To guide me back with knowledge gained
And insights to enhance our view
So, I'm able to be more complete with you.

I can't wait to be home with you and start living it!

While you Sleep

As you are sleeping now
I find peace just in knowing
How much love we share
While living, silently it goes unsaid.

With you by my side the journey is light
And when I fail, you pick me up just right
I see your beauty, it shines more each day
Today, we finally have time to share it our way.

Without distractions on this beach, it's so clear
As I look out and see vast horizons
I'm quietly grateful as our love grows wise
Because of you I can be myself and assured.

For when you wake, I again vow to show how much I care
As we grow onward together, I will not forbear.
With subtle sharing and kindness obsessed
And deep in thanks for these days are blessed.

There is no denying that I'm a lucky man!

Stages

All these chapters recorded in time
Capture an array of feelings
As travels and memories collide
With reflections sublime.

Each page its own moment
Whether for joy or sorrow brought
Occurs etched in my being
Stamped deep in my thought.

The lessons of time teach
Beyond the shadows they reach
Deep into my roots they stand
Symbols of who I am.

Are these merely stages
Of whom I once was
Or are they the foundation
Of whom I've become?

Can I embrace the stages of now?
And change results to ready
My place at the gates
By living closer to you.

Our Wedding Day (Revisited)

As I struggle at times to find the words to say
There was nothing clearer than our wedding day
As I stood there alone waiting and watching you
Come down the aisle aglow, just being you!

Every experience, poem and memory all in one
Went rushing through my head, so worth this wait!
For without Gods hand in my life's journey to you
Nothing would have ever made sense.

You gave me faith on that warm summer's night
opening new roads, I was guided by your light
And as you walk closer, I watch your eyes and smile
I melt just thinking of how great it has been
And in just a minute we will be wed.

Now its thirty years later, I look to our picture every day
I still thank God for his wisdom and guidance
For throughout my life I had been searching
And not have to worry about the proper Things to Say!

You have been the love of my life
And the path to you has been journaled
But the most fulfilling verse I've ever written
Is that *I am living it* with your love each day!

Dedications

There are several people who have influenced me over time, mostly my family. My mom Rose provided my drive as I always wanted to prove I could do something. Thank you for making me competitive. My dad Bob was kind and easy to talk to, creating fair boundaries and providing my gift of gab. His calm patience has helped level me when things weren't going well, saying it would look different the next day and he was often right.

My sisters, Marilyn and Barb each in their own ways were the glue of our family as both are emotional, deep thought provoking, and yes, competitive too. My brother Dan resembles my dad as he is always thoughtful and kind, staying clear of the competitive arm wrestling of all his siblings. All in all, our family does everything with passion and to them I am ever grateful.

I'd like to thank my friend Mark Utter for his deep friendship and guiding hand with this journey as well as the picture for the cover! Also, Jeff and Eric, along with my sisters for being my test market for material. I want to thank my other friends who were with me during my journey through the years, Jerry, Gillie, Don and Dave for the roll you all played in believing there was a better plan for my life. And one of my first girlfriends Shelly, for getting me started in writing expressions.

And finally, my wife Cheryl, for her willingness to put up with me while I reached back to the past and for her loving inspiration, coaching and editing in my pursuit. Without her support none of this would be possible. I Love You!

To my sons Brett and Alex, my wish is that your journey toward a better path is completed with more highs than lows in life. Thanks to Alex for his graphic design skills and guidance throughout this project!

A special Thank You to Tejal M.@superiar from India, who created the illustrations for this book. Her watercolor art has made my poems come to life. Her patience is greatly appreciated.